Sharing An Imagination
PARK ADVENTURE

Social Thinking Publishing, Santa Clara, California
www.socialthinking.com

Sharing An Imagination
Park Adventure

Ryan Hendrix, Kari Zweber Palmer, Nancy Tarshis, Michelle Garcia Winner

ISBN: 978-1-936943-34-0

Think Social Publishing, Inc.
404 Saratoga Avenue, Suite 200
Santa Clara, CA 95050
Tel: (408) 557-8595
Fax: (408) 557-8594

This book was printed and bound in the United States by Mighty Color Printing.
Think Social Publishing is a sole source provider.
Books may be purchased online at www.socialthinking.com.

Introduction to Storybook ⑩

Shared imagination is the ability to imagine what another person(s) is thinking, feeling, and/or pretending. Most young kids develop the ability to imagine or pretend together; it's the means by which they relate to the thoughts, feelings, and actions of others. Many children with social emotional learning challenges struggle with shared imagination, though, despite having a vivid **singular imagination**. They are able to create imaginary worlds in their own minds, but can't easily imagine what another person is thinking or pretending. To share in what someone is imagining is complex processing!

We Thinkers! Our Amazing Early Learner Curriculum!

We Thinkers! Volume 1* - *Social Explorers* and Volume 2 - *Social Problem Solvers* is an engaging Social Thinking® series designed to teach Michelle Garcia Winner's basic Social Thinking Vocabulary concepts to children ages 4-7. Each volume consists of storybooks, curricula and kid-friendly music that make core social concepts come alive for young learners. The teaching is cumulative: Volume 1 helps prime students for the deeper social concepts and activities in Volume 2.

Volume 1 explores five basic social concepts that help children learn to think about others as they learn to be part of a group: *thinking thoughts and feeling feelings, the group plan, thinking with your eyes, body in the group, and whole body listening.* Volume 2 introduces five core Social Thinking concepts related to teaching stronger executive functioning in a classroom or group setting: *hidden rules and expected/ unexpected behavior, making a smart guess, flexible versus stuck thinking, the size of a problem, and sharing an imagination.* Each storybook is aligned with a curriculum unit that breaks down these social emotional concepts into concrete, teachable segments. Adults find detailed strategies and explicit ways to engage students and foster deeper learning about each concept.

Our goal in developing the *We Thinkers!* series is to provide sequenced clear instruction to engage students in their own social emotional learning so they can become better group collaborators and problem solvers. To that end, in Volume 2 we introduce a Group Collaboration, Play and Problem Solving (GPS) scale, checklist and interactive play activities. These materials guide parents and professionals in evaluating each child's current abilities to relate to their peers and then choose from an array of interactive play activities based on their particular social learning needs.

While all children can benefit from the social emotional teaching that is at the foundation of our *We Thinkers!* series, it was specifically designed to help promote social learning in children who have solid to strong language and academic learning skills who also have social learning challenges (e.g. ASD, ADHD, twice-exceptional, behavioral challenges, etc.). However, mainstream teachers now adopt our materials for use with all students as they find them user-friendly for all.

* formerly titled *The Incredible Flexible You, Volume 1*

Teaching the Curriculum, Concepts and Activities

What does play have to do with group collaboration and classroom learning? It is well documented in the research that interactive and pretend play is the avenue through which our young children practice and perfect their social thinking and social skills. By the time children enter kindergarten it is assumed they have learned basic concepts and skills that allow them to work and learn academic concepts in a group setting.

It's tempting to think of play as simple, but it's actually a highly complex array of concepts and skills that work together simultaneously to enable a child to be successful in playing and interacting with others. Through interactive play children learn pivotal group interaction skills that will carry them through to adulthood. Play encourages the development of problem solving and conflict resolution skills, facilitates central thinking, conceptual development, perspective taking, and executive functioning.

Our multi-sensory curriculum reflects the idea that learning should be interactive and playful. Activities involve using our eyes, ears, body and brain to make important social emotional connections. Teaching within the series draws on:

- "bibliotherapy" – using the words and illustrations in storybooks to help young learners develop an understanding of self and others and elicit a therapeutic response;

- "music therapy" – using music to help foster engagement around our core social emotional concepts;

- a wide range of activities to encourage children to explore and practice each of our 10 core concepts;

- "differentiated interactive play instruction" – not all children have the same abilities to play with other children. Through our GPS scale and checklist, parents and professionals can select which play activities are best suited to the child's level.

Together, the materials provided in our *We Thinkers!* series help young learners develop the five core competencies at the heart of social and emotional learning (SEL): self-awareness, self-management, social awareness, relationship skills, and responsible decision-making. The concepts marry playful, interactive learning to Common Core, state or country standards of education around the world.

Pace Yourself and Your Kids!

The concepts in Volume 2 explore group collaboration at a deeper level and the ideas are a little more detailed to teach. To increase engagement and protect kids from becoming overwhelmed, we recommend teaching the stories in sections. While we encourage you to let your students guide you in determining the "best" places to start and stop, we've noticed in our own "test teaching" more natural breaking points in the plot and content. These sections are outlined below and are marked in the story.

Section 1, pages 1-6: Defining the concept: imagination

Section 2, pages 7-15: Defining the concept: sharing an imagination
Exploring how play is every changing and flexible

Section 3, pages 16-26: Strategy for sharing an imagination: the Tunnel of Change

Section 4, pages 27-33: Sharing an imagination to keep the play going!

The *We Thinkers!* series is available for purchase in the U.S. at www.socialthinking.com.

Evan, Ellie, Jesse and Molly are meeting at the park today.

They love to play and pretend together.

Ellie is already there.

Ellie is having fun swinging, but wants to play something while she waits for the other kids to arrive. She likes to use her imagination to pretend to be something she is not. When we imagine, we are thinking about something that isn't actually there. It might not even be real.

Sometimes Ellie imagines she is an astronaut blasting into outer space. Sometimes she imagines she is a bird flying high in the sky.

Swinging high and fast on the swings gives Ellie an idea. She can pretend the swing is something that moves fast, like a running horse! Cowgirls ride horses and Ellie loves to play cowgirl. To pretend, she thinks about what cowgirls wear, what they say, and what they do, and this gives Ellie a picture in her head.

Stop and Notice

Now Ellie is pretending she is wearing her cowboy boots and cowboy hat.
Ellie imagines that the swing is no longer a swing, it's a horse!

"Giddy up!" she exclaims.

Evan and Molly are almost at the park. They are using their imaginations too! Evan is pretending his bike is a dragon but Molly doesn't know that until he tells her. "Hey Molly, watch me fly! This bike is a dragon!"

Molly is imagining her bike is a motorcycle. "My motorcycle is faster than your dragon. Vrooom!" she yells as she speeds ahead.

"No way," says Evan. "Let's race!"

Stop and Notice

7

Molly and Evan join Ellie on the swings. "Howdy y'all!" yells Ellie.

"Get on your horses! Let's ride!"

"Ellie is pretending to ride a horse!" thinks Evan.

"Ah, Ellie must be pretending she is a cowgirl!" thinks Molly.

Evan and Molly think about cowboys and cowgirls.

Evan imagines he has a cowboy hat. Molly thinks

about a horse.

Stop and Notice

"Ye-haw!" they all shout.
They are sharing their imaginations
and pretending to ride horses together.

Jesse finally gets to the park and sees his friends on the swings. He thinks about how they pretended to be firefighters yesterday. They all had fun imagining together. He wants to do that again!

"Hey Jesse!" yells Evan. "We are pretending to ride horses!"

"Yee-haw!" adds Molly. "We are cowgirls and cowboys!"

"That sounds fun, but there aren't enough swings," Jesse says.

"Wanna play firefighters instead?" Jesse asks.

Molly and Evan think that sounds fun too.

The kids are flexible thinkers. They can change what they are playing to imagine new things!

"Yeah!" Molly says. "I'll be the firefighter and Jesse, you can be the cat I rescue from the tree."

"I don't really want to be a cat," Jesse tells her.
"I want to be a firefighter too!"
"I know!" Evan shouts. "We can all be firefighters."
"Yeah!" says Molly. Evan, Jesse and Molly share their ideas and
start to make a group plan.
"Let's pretend the playground is the fire station," Evan says.
"Yeah," Jesse agrees, "and over there is where we park our fire truck!"

Ellie thinks it would be fun to play firefighters too. She imagines herself jumping in the truck and racing off to the rescue.

Ellie is imagining, but her body is not in the group. She is not saying anything
or showing the others that she is pretending to be a firefighter.

Ellie is not sharing her imagination.

Evan, Jesse and Molly don't know that she wants to play.

Stop and Discuss

Evan, Jesse and Molly run over to the tunnel at the playground. Sometimes when they play, they pretend the playground has a magical *tunnel of change*. They start out as a boy or girl but after they crawl through the tunnel, they imagine they turn into something different!

"I'll go through the tunnel first," says Evan.

He thinks about firefighters. What do they wear? What do they do?

What do they say?

Evan crawls through the tunnel of change and when he comes out, he pretends he is now a firefighter! He imagines he is wearing a fire jacket, helmet, and big boots. Jesse and Molly know Evan is pretending to be a firefighter. Jesse will take his turn next.

Molly and Jesse go through the tunnel of change.

When they come out of the tunnel they still look like kids, but they are all imagining they are firefighters.

They are thinking about themselves and each other as firefighters holding a fire hose together. They are sharing an imagination!

"Off to the fire station!" Molly says and the kids run over to the playground. She adds, "We can wait here until we get a call from someone who needs help!" The kids imagine the playground is a fire station.

"Let's get our equipment ready," says Molly. "Firefighters need a truck. What could we use?"

"We can pretend this Frisbee is a steering wheel," says Evan.

"And this jump rope could be our hose," adds Jesse.

Molly picks up a ball. "This can be the phone," she says, "and listen... it's ringing!"

"What is your emergency?" Molly asks as she answers the phone. She pretends there is a person talking to her. "Ok! We will be right there!"

Molly turns to Jesse and Evan. "Guys, there is an emergency on 6th Street. They need our help. Let's go!"

The kids pretend to jump into the truck and speed away.

On the way to the emergency, the fire truck passes by Ellie.

"Come on Ellie! Let's go!" Evan calls out.

Ellie puts her body in the group and imagines she is on the fire truck too.

"Firefighters to the rescue!" she yells.

Now they are all imagining together, they are sharing an imagination!

Stop and Discuss

"What's the emergency?" asks Ellie.

"There is a family of turtles on 6th Street. They got stuck trying to cross the road," says Molly. "Let's go rescue them!"

The firefighters arrive on the scene. "Look!" says Evan, "there is a truck in the way. It must have stopped quickly so it didn't hit the turtles."

"Oh no," adds Ellie, "the truck was carrying balls and they are falling out everywhere!"

Firefighters to the rescue!

Evan, Ellie, Jesse and Molly pretend to collect the balls and put them back in the truck. They use their firefighter tools to help.

The firefighters work together quickly and clean up all the balls.
"Great work team!" says Ellie.

"Now we need to figure out how to rescue the turtle family!" adds Molly.
"Does anyone have an idea?"

"We could scoop them up in our helmets?" suggests Evan.

"Or use our boots," says Jesse.

"I know!" exclaims Ellie. "We could use our hose to spray a lot of water on the street."

"Yeah," says Molly, "then the turtles can swim across!"

28

Evan, Ellie, Jesse and Molly grab the hose.

They hold on together and pretend to spray the water on the street.

They imagine the water and the turtles!

"It's working!" yells Jesse. They all cheer as the turtles swim safely to the other side of the road. Firefighters to the rescue!

After a hard day of work, the firefighters drive back to the station. It's time
to go home so they run over to the tunnel of change. They crawl through,
one by one, and they imagine they are turning back into
the boys and girls they really are.

The kids say goodbye to each other as the sun sets.

They had so much fun playing and sharing their imaginations.

Together they can play and imagine anything!

Although this adventure is over,
tomorrow is another chance for sharing an imagination.